HOME

SHELLEY ROTNER & AMY GOLDBAS   Photography by SHELLEY ROTNER

M̲   Millbrook Press / Minneapolis

FOR DIANE, WITH GRATITUDE, FOR MAKING ME FEEL AT HOME —SR

FOR MIKE, JESSIE, AND JAKE. HOME IS WHERE YOU ARE. —AG

HOME IS WHERE THE HEART IS . . .

Text copyright © 2011 by Shelley Rotner and Amy Goldbas
Photographs copyright © 2011 by Shelley Rotner

Millbrook Press
A division of Lerner Publishing Group, Inc.
241 First Avenue North
Minneapolis, MN 55401 U.S.A.

Website address: www.lernerbooks.com

The following image is used with the permission of: NASA/GSFC, p. 31.

Library of Congress Cataloging-in-Publication Data

Rotner, Shelley.
    Home / by Shelley Rotner and Amy Goldbas ; photos by
Shelley Rotner.
       p.   cm. — (Shelley Rotner's early childhood library)
    ISBN: 978-0-7613-4605-0 (lib. bdg. : alk. paper)
    1. Dwellings—Juvenile literature. 2. Home—Juvenile
literature. 3. Homelessness—Juvenile literature. I. Goldbas,
Amy. II. Title.
GT172.R685 2011
640—dc22   2009051318

Manufactured in the United States of America
1 - CG - 7/15/10

Home is a place where one lives.
It is a physical structure such
as a house or an apartment.
It is a dwelling place together for family
or people living under one roof.
It is an environment offering security and happiness.

A home is more than a house.

A home is
where you live.

There are all kinds of homes.

Some are small,

and some are big.

Some are in the city,

and some are in the country.

Some are by the water.

And some move around.

A home gives you shelter.

It is also a place where you should feel safe.

At home, you can love and be loved.

At home,
you can
learn and work.

At home, you can feel happy

or sad.

At home, you can play.

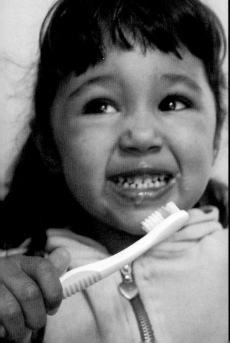

And at home,
you can wash and sleep.

Some people don't have homes
even though they are
just like you and me.

Many people
help those
in their
community
who are
homeless.

People and their homes make
a community.

And communities
make the world—one big home
for everyone!

DID YOU KNOW?

- People who do not have a home are called homeless.
- A homeless person has no safe place to live.
- In our country about 750,000 people do not have a place to live.
- Homelessness happens for many reasons to all kinds of people everywhere regardless of skin color, religion, gender, or age.
- Some people who are homeless may have lost their homes in natural disasters like hurricanes, fires, or floods.
- Others might not have a job or make enough money to pay for a place to live.
- There are people and organizations in your community that help the homeless.

YOU CAN HELP—HERE'S HOW:

- Treat all people with respect no matter where they live.
- Volunteer with your family to cook or serve a meal at an organization that helps homeless people.
- Collect blankets, hats, gloves, socks, toothbrushes, towels, and other items needed by organizations that aid the homeless.

PARENTS AND TEACHERS, FOR MORE INFORMATION, PLEASE VISIT:

http://www.naeh.org

http://www.mnhomelesscoalition.org/resources/curriculum

http://www.serve.org/nche (National Center for Homeless Education)